THOMAS CRANE PUBLIC LIBRARY
QUINCY MASS
CITY APPROPRIATION

PORCUPINES

Jen Green

Grolier
an imprint of
SCHOLASTIC
www.scholastic.com/librarypublishing

Published 2008 by Grolier
An imprint of Scholastic Library Publishing
Old Sherman Turnpike, Danbury,
Connecticut 06816

© 2008 Grolier

All rights reserved. Except for use in
a review, no part of this book may be
reproduced, stored in a retrieval system,
or transmitted in any form, or by any
means, electronic or mechanical, including
photocopying, recording, or otherwise,
without prior permission of Grolier.

For The Brown Reference Group plc
Project Editor: Jolyon Goddard
Copy-editors: Ann Baggaley, Lisa Hughes
Picture Researcher: Clare Newman
Designers: Jeni Child, Lynne Ross,
    Sarah Williams
Managing Editor: Bridget Giles

Volume ISBN-13: 978-0-7172-6278-6
Volume ISBN-10: 0-7172-6278-2

**Library of Congress
Cataloging-in-Publication Data**

Nature's children. Set 3.
    p. cm.
  Includes bibliographical references and
index.
  ISBN 13: 978-0-7172-8082-7
  ISBN 10: 0-7172-8082-9
  1. Animals--Encyclopedias, Juvenile. I.
  Grolier Educational (Firm)
  QL49.N384 2008
  590.3--dc22
                                    2007031568

Printed and bound in China

PICTURE CREDITS

Front Cover: **Superstock**: Age Fotostock.

Back Cover: **Alamy**: Image State;
Photolibrary.com: J. and C. Sohns;
Photos.com; **Shutterstock**: Sara
Robinson.

Corbis: Tom Brakefield 17, Daniel J. Cox 46,
Frank Lukasseck 26–27, D. Robert and Lorri
Franz 42, Paul A. Souders 34; **Nature PL**:
Tony Heald 33, Larry Michael 6, Lynn M. Stone
14, 30, Dave Watts 38; **Photolibrary.com**:
Tim Jackson 10, 37, Brian Kenney 9, Brandon
Randy 18; **Shutterstock**: 29, Murie Lasure
4, 13, Sara Robinson 22; **Still Pictures**:
BIOS/Jean-Paul Chatagnon 5, Martin Harvey
2–3, 41, Thomas D. Mangelsen 21;
Superstock: Age Fotostock 45.

Contents

Fact File: Porcupines 4

We Are Rodents 7

Porcupine Types 8

Suitable Homes 11

Clever Climbers 12

On the Ground 15

Plant Food 16

Sharp Teeth 19

A Craving for Salt 20

Snoozing All Day 23

Nighttime Feeders 24

Super Sniffers 25

Feature Photo 26–27

Winter Survival 28

Splitting Hairs 31

Bristly Armor 32

I'm Warning You 35

Deadly Weapons 36

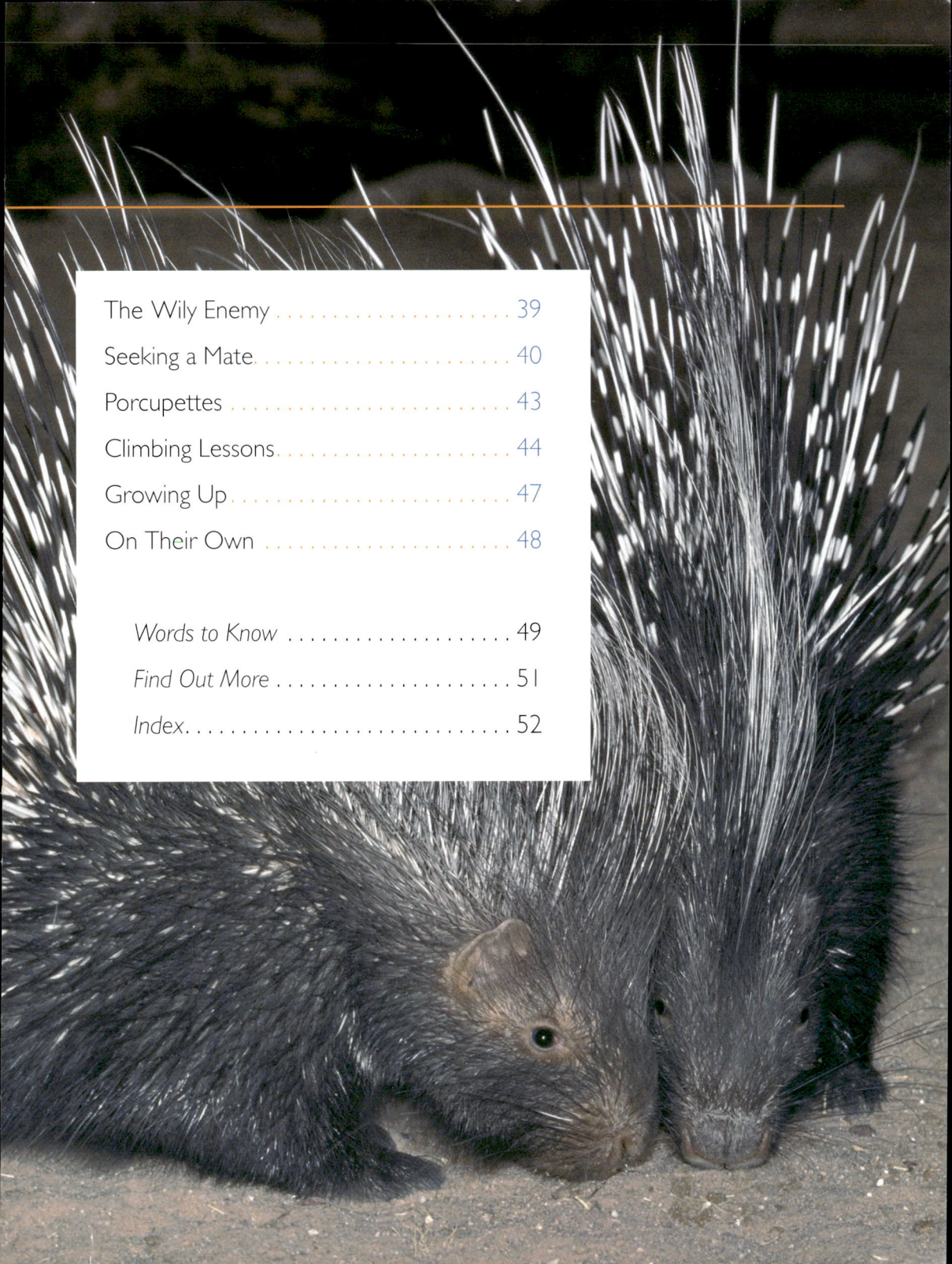

The Wily Enemy 39
Seeking a Mate 40
Porcupettes 43
Climbing Lessons 44
Growing Up 47
On Their Own 48

Words to Know 49
Find Out More 51
Index 52

FACT FILE: Porcupines

Class	Mammals (Mammalia)
Order	Rodents (Rodentia)
Families	New World porcupines (Erethizontidae) and Old World porcupines (Hystricidae)
Genera	8 genera worldwide
Species	23 species worldwide, including the North American porcupine (*Erethizon dorsatum*)
World distribution	North American porcupine lives only in North America; other porcupines live in South America, Africa, Asia, and southern Europe
Habitat	Forest, scrubland, and open country
Distinctive physical characteristics	The sturdy body is covered with long hair and defensive quills; the head is large and the legs are shortish; the long front teeth are colored orange
Habits	Porcupines mostly live alone. When alarmed they turn around and raise their quills, while shaking their tail
Diet	Twigs, tree bark, leaves, shrubs, and flowers

Introduction

What animal is pricklier than a pincushion? It's a porcupine. Porcupines have more than 30,000 long, sharp prickles, called **quills**, all over their body. They use these as weapons to defend themselves from enemies. Porcupines are fat and slow moving, which would seem to make them easy prey for hunting animals. But because of their sharp quills, most **predators** leave them alone. Porcupines are found in many countries, including North America, South America, Africa, and Asia. Some are large, some are small, but they are all very prickly!

This is a North American porcupine.

Huge teeth and strong jaw muscles make gnawing tough food easy work for a porcupine.

We Are Rodents

Porcupines are sometimes called porkies or quill-pigs, but they are not related to pigs. Nor are they related to two other types of prickly animals—hedgehogs and spiny anteaters.

In fact, porcupines belong to the **rodent** family. Rodents are the largest group of mammals, with more than 2,000 species, or types. Rats, mice, and squirrels are rodents. So are gophers, beavers, and woodchucks. Within this huge family, the porcupines' closest cousins are the guinea pigs, which are also called **cavies**. Other relatives include fluffy chinchillas and a giant, water-loving rodent from South America called the capybara.

Like all rodents, porcupines have two long, chisel-shaped front teeth called **incisors**, which are perfect for gnawing plant food.

Porcupine Types

Porcupines live in many different parts of the world, including the Americas or "New World." There are also porcupines living in Africa and southern Asia—these are called "Old World" porcupines. There are 23 different species of porcupines.

The North American porcupine is one of the largest species. In fact, it's the second-largest North American rodent, after the beaver. Most North American male porcupines measure about three feet (1 m) from snout to tail-tip. They weigh about 12 pounds (5.5 kg) and are around the size of a large house cat. The females are smaller. One of the smallest porcupines is the long-tailed porcupine of Southeast Asia, which has a body just a foot (30 cm) long.

Most porcupines are stout animals with a large head and shortish legs. However, long-tailed porcupines are longer and slimmer, with a shape more like that of a rat.

This young tree porcupine lives in South America.

These African porcupines are quite at home on the ground.

Suitable Homes

Porcupines can be found living in all sorts of places, including forests, grasslands, deserts, and even high in the mountains. South American porcupines prefer to live in dense forests. North American porcupines are less picky. They can be found in most parts of North America, except for northern Canada and the southeastern United States. Porcupines mainly keep to woods and forests, but they also turn up in dry scrublands, on the plains, and even on the bleak, windswept tundra.

Unlike the porcupines found in Africa and Asia, American porcupines mostly dwell in trees. African and Asian species keep their feet firmly on the ground.

Clever Climbers

Each type of porcupine has special features that help to make it comfortable in its surroundings. North American porcupines spend most of their time in the treetops. Their broad feet and sharp claws make them perfectly equipped for climbing. To get up a tree, they dig their long, curving claws into the bark. They then haul themselves up with their front feet, while pushing with their back feet. The hairless soles of their feet have little ridges, similar to the ridges on a car tire, which help the porcupine to grip the bark.

    The North American porcupine uses its broad tail as a prop while climbing. The underside of the tail is covered with stiff, bristly hairs that also grip the bark. Some South American porcupines have a flexible tail, similar to a monkey's tail. This type of tail acts like a fifth limb, curling around branches. These porcupines can even hang by their tail from a branch to reach food.

The North American porcupine is a slow but steady climber. It is sometimes seen edging its way up trees more than 60 feet (18 m) above the ground.

Down among the leaves on the forest floor, this porcupine watches for any sign of danger.

On the Ground

North American porcupines spend time on the ground as they move between trees or return to their den. They climb down trees tail first, reversing the movements they used going up.

On the ground, the porcupine waddles along on its short legs. If threatened by an enemy, it can break into a clumsy gallop. Most often it heads for the safety of the nearest tree.

Porcupines usually live beside rivers, streams, or lakes. These prickly rodents actually love the water and are quite good swimmers. Their hollow quills are filled with air. Together the quills act a little like a life jacket, helping the porcupine to float.

Plant Food

Porcupines are **herbivores**, or plant eaters. They eat all sorts of plant foods, including leaves, flowers, shoots, and tender grass. In the fall, they munch on any nuts, berries, and seeds that they can find.

A porcupine's favorite treat is tree bark, and the juicy layer just beneath the bark, called the **cambium**. Sometimes porcupines gnaw off whole branches, which then crash to the ground. These fallen branches provide food for animals such as deer and rabbits—creatures that lack the porcupine's climbing skills.

Porcupines are unpopular with some people because of the damage they do to trees. These animals eat so much bark that they even smell like sawdust or old wood.

Flowers are a spring or summer treat for an Old World porcupine.

If a porcupine's incisors don't wear down fast enough, the ever-growing teeth can stop the animal from feeding easily.

Sharp Teeth

Porcupines need strong, sharp teeth in order to bite off chunks of bark and mash up stringy grass and leaves. Their wedge-shaped front incisor teeth are just right for nibbling. These teeth keep growing throughout the porcupine's life. They don't usually get too long, because the porcupine wears them down by gnawing all the time.

The fronts of the teeth are covered with a tough, orange-colored coating that protects them. The backs don't have the coating, so they wear down more quickly. This keeps the teeth chisel-shaped and very sharp.

As well as the incisors, the porcupine has 16 other broad, flat teeth in its mouth. These are used to crush and grind tough plants to a pulp.

A Craving for Salt

If there's one thing porcupines go crazy for, it's salt. They love anything salty—and that includes objects on which salty human sweat has dried, such as the handles of tools. People camping in forests are often disturbed in the night by loud gnawing sounds. The sleepy campers awake to find a porcupine gnawing at their picnic table. These animals have even been known to eat sweaty sneakers left outside tents.

Signposts, canoe paddles, and steering wheels have all been gnawed by porcupines looking to satisfy their salt cravings. Their love of salt sometimes attracts them to human settlements, which these shy creatures usually avoid. They have even been known to break into houses to chew salty patches of furniture, such as the arms of chairs.

A porcupine on the trail of salt peers hopefully through a window.

A tree branch is as good as a soft bed to a porcupine.

Snoozing All Day

Porcupines are **nocturnal.** They rest during the day and they are active at night. They spend all day snoozing, usually in the fork of a tree. Here they are safe from ground-based predators such as coyotes. Some porcupines bed down inside a hollow log, cave, or crevice in the rocks.

Porcupines are difficult to spot. Their light brown fur helps them to blend in perfectly with the tree branches upon which they rest. A resting porcupine can easily be mistaken for an old bird's nest or a clump of dead leaves caught on a branch. If you think you see a porcupine, never be tempted to climb up to check. An angry porcupine that has been suddenly awakened might back toward you, raising its quills and lashing a tail full of dangerous spines.

Nighttime Feeders

When the sun goes down and many animals are ready to sleep, including humans, porcupines wake up and go hunting. These solitary animals look for food on their own.

In the course of its nighttime wandering, a porcupine might visit a lush meadow, where it will munch leaves and flowers to its heart's content. A tree with tasty bark is also a favorite meal for the porcupine. In summer, a porcupine might wade or swim across a pond to feast on delicious water lilies.

If a porcupine finds a good feeding spot, it will return night after night. As time goes on, it wears a little trail to its favorite feeding place. This trail is like the porcupine's own private highway.

Super Sniffers

Porcupines find their food mostly by using their keen sense of smell. A hungry porcupine wanders along with its nose to the ground, making loud sniffing noises. Or it might sit back on its hind legs to sniff the air, hoping to catch the scent of fresh leaves. At close quarters, the long whiskers on its snout help the porcupine to feel its way toward food.

Porcupines are very **nearsighted**. This means their small, beady eyes are only good at seeing objects at close range. Since they hunt at night when it's dark, keen eyesight is not very important. They have been known to stumble upon people—practically bumping right into them—if they haven't picked up their scent.

A porcupine sleeps during the day. In the evening, it wakes up and goes looking for food.

27

Winter Survival

Some mammals, such as woodchucks, spend the winter months in a deep sleep called **hibernation**. It makes sense to save energy by sleeping when food is scarce. However, porcupines have no trouble finding food all year round, so they don't hibernate. In winter, they mostly feed on pine needles, or on the juicy cambium layer found just below the tree bark.

In the worst winter weather, a porcupine might take shelter in a cave, an old animal burrow, or even a quiet corner of a barn. However, the harsh winter weather is no match for these hardy animals. Most porcupines spend whole winter months just sitting in a tree. To them, the tree is a bedroom and a refrigerator rolled into one. They have a comfortable place to sleep and plenty of food to eat. These tough animals can cope with howling winds, thick snow, and bitter cold.

Snow doesn't bother a porcupine because it can always find food.

29

Porcupine hair was once used by some Native American tribes to make their traditional headdresses.

Splitting Hairs

Porcupines have not one, not two, but three different types of hairs on their body. In fall, the animal grows a dense layer of soft, fine underfur. The underfur traps air next to the porcupine's skin, which keeps the animal warm throughout the winter. In spring, most of this fine, fluffy fur drops out again.

On top of the underfur is a layer of long, coarse hairs called **guard hairs**. These hairs repel rain and snow to keep the porcupine dry. The outer fur is many shades of brown, which helps the animal hide in the forest. This natural disguise, called **camouflage**, makes it more difficult for predators to spot the porcupine.

The porcupine is most famous for its third type of hair—its quills. It might be hard to believe, but these sharp, needlelike spines are actually made of hardened hair.

Bristly Armor

A porcupine's spines cover its whole body. Only its face, belly, paws, and the underside of its tail are quill-free. The long, hollow quill shafts are creamy-white with brown or black tips. These varied, earth-toned colors conceal the porcupine as it climbs through the forest.

The North American porcupine has quills up to 3 inches (10 cm) long. Some Old World species have much longer spines. The crested African porcupine has black-and-white quills up to a foot (30 cm) long.

The point of each quill is rough and covered with tiny **barbs**. If a porcupine jabs a quill into another animal, the barbs lie flat as the quill pierces the skin. But if anyone tries to pull the quill back out, the barbs open up like an umbrella. That makes removing a quill very difficult— and painful!

The African crested porcupine has much longer quills than its New World cousins.

A porcupine turns its back in an effort to frighten an enemy with its quills.

34

I'm Warning You

Most of the time a porcupine's quills are hardly visible, because they lie flat under the long guard hairs. But if danger threatens, the porcupine raises its quills, in the same way an angry dog raises the hairs on its neck and back.

In most porcupines, the longest quills are on the back and neck. Because of this the porcupine spins around as it prepares to defend itself. It shows its rear end to the enemy, while arching its back and lowering its head. This helps to protect the quill-less parts of its body, which would be easier to attack.

The porcupine warns enemies that it is armed and dangerous by lashing its tail and stamping its feet. Some porcupines make a scary rattling sound with their quills. Any animal that ignores these danger signs is likely to get hurt.

Deadly Weapons

A porcupine's quills are only loosely attached to its skin, especially on the tail. When the animal lashes its tail from side to side, some quills may come loose and fly through the air. People used to think that porcupines could fire their quills on purpose, but this is not true.

Animals that come too close are likely to end up with a noseful of quills. This is painful and can also be dangerous. If the quills get stuck in an animal's mouth or throat, it may not be able to eat. Predators, such as coyotes, have been known to starve to death after being pricked by a porcupine. Most predators recognize the danger, and know to steer clear.

A young lion contemplates whether to risk attacking a pair of African porcupines.

37

A fisher can crouch down low and move quickly around a porcupine to attack its face.

38

The Wily Enemy

A porcupine's spiny armor scares off most predators, including foxes and coyotes. In Africa, even big cats such as lions and cheetahs think twice before attacking these well-defended animals. But in North America, a wily hunter called the fisher knows the best way to defeat a porcupine.

Fishers are fierce, clever animals related to weasels. The crafty hunter circles around the porcupine, before darting in and flipping it onto its back. It can then easily attack the porcupine's quill-less belly.

In many parts of the world, people hunt porcupines for their meat and for their quills, which can be used as needles. Human hunters usually kill the animal with a blow to its head. The quills can then be burned off in a fire. Porcupines were an important source of food to Native Americans and early pioneers.

Seeking a Mate

Porcupines are happy to be alone for most of the year. But when the breeding season comes around in the fall, the lone porcupines begin seeking a mate. The male porcupine wanders through the forest, singing a loud mating song, made up of grunts, whines, hums, and chatterings.

If a female hears his song, she joins in with her own hums and whistles. When the pair meet up, they do a little dance together. They may rear up on their hind legs as they move closer, humming all the while. Then they sniff each other and put their paws on each other's shoulders. They may even touch noses. That's dating, porcupine-style.

This courting pair are African crested porcupines.

41

For the first few weeks of a young porcupine's life its mother stays close by.

Porcupettes

In spring or early summer, the female porcupine looks for a sheltered spot, such as a clump of bushes, to use as a nursery. There, about seven months after mating, she gives birth to a single baby. Baby porcupines are sometimes called **porcupettes**.

Some baby mammals are blind, hairless, and helpless for weeks after birth—but not baby porcupines. The porcupette's eyes open immediately after birth. It is covered with soft black hair, complete with tiny quills, which harden just a few hours after its birth. The baby soon looks like a smaller model of its mother. And just half an hour after being born, it is able to stand and walk on its small, sturdy feet.

Climbing Lessons

Male porcupines are not much help when it comes to raising the young. The mother porcupine is left to raise the baby on her own.

When the porcupette is just a few days old, the mother gives it the first lesson in the tricky art of climbing. She begins by climbing into a tree and calling for the baby to join her. As the porcupette digs its tiny claws into the bark and starts to climb, she moves a little higher. Slowly, the baby follows her up to the top of the tree.

The baby may take a few tumbles. But before long it becomes a skilled climber. When not feeding or practicing its climbing skills, the porcupette snoozes in the safety of thick shrubs or a hollow log.

Young porcupines can climb trees easily within a week or two of birth.

45

A porcupette eats a flower.

46

Growing Up

At birth, the baby porcupine is equipped with eight tiny teeth, including its front gnawing teeth. At first, like all baby mammals, the porcupette needs only its mother's milk to survive. But at the age of just two weeks old, it begins to eat solid food as well. It nibbles on tender shoots and grass. The porcupette stops drinking its mother's milk at six or seven weeks old. This is called **weaning**.

Like most young mammals, porcupettes are naturally playful. These babies rarely have a brother or sister—but if one porcupette meets another, the two will play together. They might have a mock fight or chase each other around in circles. Baby porcupines like to play by themselves, too. They have been seen doing a funny, stiff-legged walk, or spinning around like a prickly top.

On Their Own

The mother porcupine stays with her baby for about two months. Even if the pair are in different trees, they stay within earshot. The mother keeps in touch by chattering and hooting to her baby. She calls to the youngster when it is time to wake from its daytime sleep, or to encourage it to climb a tree.

By fall of its first year, the young porcupine is ready to leave its mother and head off on its own. If it has learned its survival lessons well, it could live to about nine years old. Young female porcupines sometimes have a baby of their own at 18 months old. The young males don't usually become a father until they are about two and a half years old.

Words to Know

Barbs The little points on the end of a porcupine's quill that help it stick in an animal's flesh.

Cambium A juicy layer below the bark of trees.

Camouflage Color and patterns on an animal's coat that make it hard to see against its surroundings.

Cavies Mammals belonging to the group of rodents that includes guinea pigs. Porcupines are cavies.

Guard hairs The long, coarse hairs of an animal's coat that repel rain and snow.

Herbivores Plant-eating animals.

Hibernation A deep sleep lasting through the winter. Animals save energy by hibernating.

Incisors   The sharp, chisel-shaped front teeth that rodents use to nibble their food.

Nearsighted   When an animal or person can see things clearly only at close range.

Nocturnal   The behavior of animals that wake at night and rest during the day.

Porcupettes   Young porcupines.

Predators   Animals that hunt other animals for food.

Quills   The sharp spines that cover most of the porcupine's body, and which are used to ward off attack.

Rodent   An animal in the group of mammals that includes rats, mice, squirrels, porcupines, and guinea pigs.

Weaning   When a young animal stops drinking its mother's milk and eats solid food.

Find Out More

Books

Jango-Cohen, J. *Porcupines*. Animals, Animals. New York: Benchmark Books, 2005.

Schaefer, L. M. *Porcupines*. Tiny-Spiny Animals. Portsmouth, New Hampshire: Heinemann, 2003.

Web sites

North American Porcupine
www.enchantedlearning.com/subjects/mammals/rodent/Porcupineprintout.shtml
Information and a printout to color in.

Porcupine
animals.nationalgeographic.com/animals/mammals/porcupine.html
Facts, photos, and sounds.

Index

A, B
African porcupines 8, 10, 11, 32, 33, 37, 41
American porcupines 8, 11, 12, 15, 32
Asian porcupines 8, 11
barbs 32
birth 43, 47
breeding season 40

C, D
cambium 16, 28
camouflage 31
claws 12, 44
climbing 12, 13, 15, 16, 44, 45, 48
coloring 31, 32, 43
dancing 40
defense 5, 35

E, F
eyes 25, 43
feet 12, 35, 43
females 8, 40, 43, 44, 48
food 7, 12, 16, 24, 25, 28, 29, 47
fur 23, 31

G, H, I
gnawing 6, 7, 16, 19, 20, 47
guard hairs 31, 35
guinea pigs 7
habitat 11, 15
hair 12, 30, 31, 43
herbivores 16
hibernation 28
hunting 24, 25
incisors 7, 18, 19

L, M, N
legs 8, 15, 25, 40
length 8
life span 48
long-tailed porcupine 8
males 8, 40, 44, 48
mammals 7, 28
mating 40, 43
mating song 40
milk 47
nearsightedness 25
New World porcupines 8

O, P, Q
Old World porcupines 8, 17, 32
paws 40
play 47
porcupettes 42, 43, 44, 46, 47, 48
predators 5, 23, 36, 39
quills 5, 15, 23, 30, 31, 32, 33, 34, 35, 36, 39, 43

R, S, T
rodents 7, 8
salt 20, 21
sleep 23, 27, 28, 44, 48
smell 25
species 7, 8, 11
swimming 15, 24
tail 8, 12, 35, 36
teeth 6, 7, 18, 19, 23, 47
tree bark 12, 19, 16, 24, 28, 44
tree porcupine 9

U, W
underfur 31
weaning 47
weight 8
whiskers 25

CC

THOMAS CRANE PUBLIC LIBRARY
3 1641 0082 2195 8

Central Children's